Fun Horse Facts for Kids

Jacquelyn Elnor Johnson

www.CrimsonHillBooks.com

First edition, May 2022.
Second edition, January 2024.

Cataloguing in Publication Data

Johnson, Jacquelyn Elnor

Fun Horse Facts for Kids

Description: Crimson Hill Books trade paperback edition | Nova Scotia, Canada

ISBN:	978-1-990291-73-9 (Paperback - Amazon)
BISAC:	JNF003110 Juvenile Nonfiction: Animals - Horses JNF003220 Juvenile Nonfiction: Animals - Animal Welfare JNF054170 Juvenile Nonfiction: Sports & Recreation - Equestrian
THEMA:	SK - Equestrian & animal sports YNNJ24 - Children's / Teenage general interest: Ponies and horses WNGH - Horses and ponies: general interest

Record available at https://www.bac-lac.gc.ca/eng/Pages/home.aspx

Book design: Jesse Johnson

Crimson Hill Books
(a division of)
Crimson Hill Products Inc.
Lawrencetown, Nova Scotia
Canada

Crimson Hill
Books

A happy and friendly horse.

These two guys are showing that they'd like to know you!

Do you know horses?

If your fondest wish is to have a horse of your own, or you've already made that dream come true, you probably already know a lot about them.

They're beautiful, friendly and intelligent.

We prize them for their strength, power and the work they do for us.

We also love them because they like us. They're always happy to see their owners.

Though today most horses live indoors in their stalls and stables, they'd always much rather be outside with their herd, even in cold weather. Their second-most-favourite thing to do is spend time with you, perhaps on a trail ride with other riders, or in a riding lesson, or competing at a Pony Club or Gymkhana event.

Horses are the animal you need if you want to travel where no roads go. They are beautiful to see, interesting to watch and fun to get to know. Like some other animals that live with humans, such as dogs and cats, they each have their own distinct personality.

Horses also have secrets. These are odd and quirky fun facts about them. That's what this book is all about. Once you've read it, you'll know more about the secrets of horses' lives than most other owners and riders know, even some of the most experienced people in the horse-loving world!

Horse Fun Fact:

Horses can't bend their backs.

Young competitors at a Pony Club event. Even though it's called Pony Club, horses are allowed, but all competitors have to be younger than 21 years old.

A horse isn't just a tall pony

Ponies don't grow up to be horses. Ponies are ponies for all of their lives. Although sometimes horses might be called "ponies," that tends to be a term of affection. Horses and ponies are different in how they look and in their personality.

A pony is a type of horse. All horses, including ponies, are in the species named Equus caballus. They share their family tree.

There are more than 400 registered breeds of modern horses. They live almost everywhere in the world except the coldest places where there is no grass for them to eat, such as the High Arctic and Antarctica.

There are two basic things to know about all horses. Once you know these two things, you'll understand almost everything about who they are and why they behave the way they do.

1. Horses are a prey animal.
2. Horses are a herd animal.

All animals are either predator animals or prey animals. The predators are the hunters. The prey animals are who they hunt.

Vultures, Sharks, Tigers and all the other types of cats, snakes and humans are all predators. We predators all kill other animals to eat them.

Even though they're big and strong, horses are prey animals. So are deer, sheep, songbirds, elephants and giraffes. Prey animals usually eat plants or plant products, such as seeds.

Prey animals are always watching out for their predators. They're always ready to run or fly away if they can or fight if they have to.

Most prey animals live in family groups because they need each other for protection. A family group of horses is called a herd, or a string of horses if you live in Australia. Herds usually have a lead mare. She's called this because she is responsible for leading the herd to food and fresh water. There's also a lead stallion, who is the herd bodyguard, making sure everyone stays safe. Mares along with their babies or youngsters make up the rest of the herd.

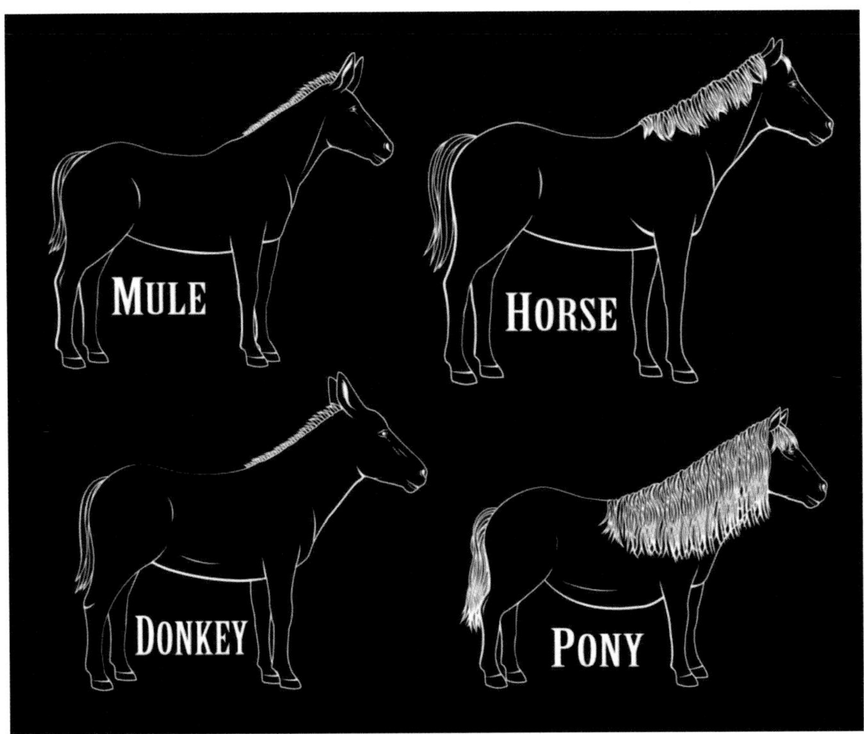

Horses are social. They live in herds for security, comfort and companionship.

Is it a horse? Or a pony?

Do you know the difference between horses and ponies?

It's not always easy to tell, just by sight. And sometimes, an animal that is actually a horse might be called a pony. One example of this is in the game of polo. The game is played with riders mounted on polo ponies. Even though they're always called "polo ponies," polo mounts are always horses.

Ponies are usually smaller, shorter and lighter than horses, but not always. There are some breeds of horses that are usually, or always smaller than some breeds of ponies. Miniature horses are a true horse, yet they are always smaller than any pony.

Both horse babies and pony babies are called foals. They look the same, except that pony foals are smaller.

Horses take longer to grow up to being adults than ponies do. Some horses aren't fully grown until they are six or seven years old, even though all horses and ponies are called adults at age four.

Although horses are bigger and heavier, they aren't always stronger, for their size, than ponies.

Ponies have a longer, and often bushier, mane and tail than horses do.

Horses have a longer muzzle and a sleeker body shape than ponies. Horses can run faster and some breeds have more endurance to do work than ponies do.

Horses are big eaters. Adjusted for their size, ponies eat half as much as horses eat.

Ponies have heavier bones than horses do and tougher hooves. Ponies also live longer than horses do, on average.

Horse Fun Fact:

Horses have 205 bones in their bodies. That's one less bone than humans have.

Donkeys, Mules and Zebras are close relatives of Horses.

Horsey Cousins

Close cousins to the entire horse family, including ponies, are:

- Donkeys – Very friendly, they like to be pets and make good companions for horses.
- Mules – Known for being strong and easy-going, mules are used to carry loads and pull wagons.
- Zebras – Newborn zebras can stand six minutes after they're born. Wild zebras live only in Eastern and Southern Africa and are endangered.

More distant cousins, but still related to horses, are:

- Rhinoceros – Wild Rhinos live only in parts of Africa and Asia.
- Tapirs – Like a wild Pig, Tapirs live in parts of Central America and South-east Asia.

What do all these horse cousins have in common? The answer is in their toes. They all have an odd number of toes, unlike most mammals, and people, who have an even number of toes. There are only 16 animals in existence today that have an odd number of toes.

Is a Zebra just a striped horse?

Zebras and horses belong to the same family, called Equidae, but they are different species.

Zebras look like horses, but there are many ways they are different. They are smaller, weigh less and run more slowly than horses. They aren't interested in being tamed or ridden by humans.

They have stiff manes that stand up like a mohawk haircut. Their tails are shorter than a horse's, but their ears are larger, more like a donkey's ears.

Horses have coats that can be several colours, but zebras always have a black and white striped coat. No two zebras have exactly the same pattern on their coats. Like human fingerprints, each zebra's coat is unique.

Zebras can run 65 kilometres, or 40 miles per hour.

Zebras live only in Africa, where they first appeared four million years ago.

Early horses

There have been horses on earth for about the last 55 million years. The very earliest horses, called

Hyracotherium, were small and probably timid creatures. They were about the size of a modern Labrador Retriever.

Over millions of years, horses grew taller and stronger. Some of their toes vanished, since they no longer needed them. Today, horses are running on what was originally their middle toe.

Horses changed very gradually, over millions of years, from forest creatures who ate tree leaves to living on the plains and eating grasses.

People didn't show up on earth until maybe five or six million years ago. We know that ancient people knew horses, because there are horses painted on cave walls in Europe. These paintings were created about 36,000 years ago.

About 15,000 years ago, Equus ferus lived almost everywhere on earth. Horses weren't tamed for riding, though, until about 6,000 years ago. That probably happened at several places in Asia, all around the same time.

By that time, very mysteriously, all the horses in North America and Australia had vanished. They became rare in most other places. It might have been that there wasn't enough food and water. Or they had too many predators. Or perhaps it was a major disaster, such as a period of global warming.

Horse Fun Fact:

There are about 70 million horses in the world.

People bred big, strong horses to do jobs, like pulling sleighs.

Why horses got big

Horses got big when there was plenty of food and being big helped their species survive. With lots of grass to eat, and not too many enemies like wolves, lions and snakes, horses got bigger over the centuries and there were more of them. Eventually, they spread around the world.

In Africa, some of them started having black and white stripes. Perhaps this was because the stripes served as camouflage, where they live. Today, we call them zebras.

Elsewhere, another group changed to be shorter, tougher, have big ears and not be very interested in

This Clydesdale team of working horses is pulling a field tiller.

running. Now we know them as donkeys.

People bred horses to have certain traits that were useful to the people. People needed horses to be strong for riding into battle or pulling carriages, or as pit ponies in coal mines.

Horse breeds

Horse breeds are usually named for where they come from, such as the gentle Hanoverian from Hanover, Germany or the high-stepping Tennessee Walking Horse, from the United States.

Based on their personality, and what jobs people need

them to do, horses are divided into three groups. These groups are called the Hot Bloods, the Cold Bloods and the Warmbloods.

Every horse is a mammal, just as humans are. This means they and we are warm-blooded. The blood that flows through our bodies is warm. These names for groups of horses isn't about their blood temperature. It's just what they're called in the horse world.

Hot Bloods, sometimes also called Light Horses or Riding Horses, are all spirited, bold and fast learners. They are prized for their speed and endurance, sensitivity and energy. They tend to be slim, long-legged and agile. Some Hot Blood breeds are Arabian, Turkoman and Thoroughbred.

Cold Bloods are strong, muscular and move slowly. They have great strength and endurance, working for hours without getting tired. They are quieter and calmer, bred to be patient workers pulling heavy wagon loads or carriages. Some Cold Blood breeds are the Shire Horse, Percheron, Friesian, Clydesdale and Belgian.

Warmbloods, were bred by crossing Hot Bloods and Cold Bloods to create good horses for riding. They are calmer than Hot Bloods, but more athletic than the Cold Bloods. Some Warmblood breeds are Irish Sport Horses, Dutch Warmblood, Trakehner and American Quarter Horse. Standardbred is a Warmblood, and also the fastest breed in harness racing in the world.

Horse Fun Fact:

Horses can't breathe through their mouths.

A rodeo competitor and his pinto horse. In horse sports, both the horse and the rider are the competitors.

Oriental breeds aren't from the Orient

The Orient is another name for Asia, sometimes used to refer only to Eastern Asian countries such as China and Japan.

The ancestors of the breeds we call Oriental breeds today didn't come from The Orient. Instead, they are Hot Bloods brought from the Middle East and North Africa to England. Why were these smaller, high-spirited and fast horses so desirable that breeders paid to import them to England?

It was because the Oriental traits made it possible to bred better, faster and stronger horses for light cavalry horses. Though Orientals look as sleek as Thoroughbreds, they have more endurance.

When tank units finally replaced mounted soldiers (this didn't happen until the 1940s and World War II) the Oriental breeds continued to earn their feed and our admiration as race horses. Modern Oriental breeds are Arabians, Akhal-Tekes and Barb horses.

Coat colours

Horses can have a coat that is gray, pale gold, rusty red, reddish-brown or black. They can have dots, or colour patterns with two colours. Here are the names for horse colours:

Dun – A dun horse is mostly a lighter version of the colour of their lower legs, mane and tail. Duns are

Totally white horses are fairly rare for most breeds. This one is gray, but could turn a lighter colour when he is older.

rare in Thoroughbreds and Arabians, but more common in other breeds.

Chestnut – This is the most common horse colour and shows up in almost every breed. It is a caramel colour, with darker or lighter mane and tail.

Bay – A bay horse is reddish-brown or brown, with a darker or black mane, tail, ear edges and lower legs. Bays are common in most horse breeds.

Pinto – A horse that has large areas of white and any other colour is a pinto.

Leopard – A white horse with black spots. Also called an Appaloosa.

Palomino – A gold or yellow horse with a cream or white mane and tail.

A horse of a different colour

A foal that is born black could be gray, or even white, as an adult. Lipizzan is a breed that is known for always doing this. They're born black and they slowly turn white. It's very rare for a Lipizzan to be born black or bay and stay that way.

Lipizzans aren't the only horses of a different colour. Over their lifetime, almost every horse changes colour. All foals are born a pale colour. Their coat changes, usually getting darker, when they lose their baby coats. This happens when they're three or four months old.

The skin colour under a horse's coat could be black or pink. Their skin colour never changes. It will stay their skin birth colour for all their life.

Horses that are born gray can be dark gray or black when they grow up. Or, if they are born black, they might be gray later on and might be almost completely white by the time they're in their teens.

Many breeds have a darker version of their usual coat colour when they're wearing their winter coat. Maybe that's so they stand out more against the snow.

This chestnut horse has an unusual bald face and even more unusual blue eyes. Most horses' eyes are brown or black.

Horse Faces

Some horses have white on their faces. But what pattern of white?

STAR means they have a round white spot between their eyes.

BLAZE is a long white mark down the middle of their face.

SKINNY BLAZE is a thin white stripe down their face.

SNIP means they've got just a little white mark on their nose.

BALD FACED sounds like they've got no hair on their face, but that's not true. What it does mean is their face is mostly white or entirely white.

Horses can recognize people in photos

Imagine that you're given a photo of a person and, maybe a week or two later, they walk past you somewhere. Would you recognize them right away, just by sight?

Maybe you would. Some people are very good at this skill, which is called face recognition. Other people aren't so good. Or they just can't do it.

But horses can! This was the stunning discovery of an experiment done in 2018 at the Universities of Sussex and Portsmouth in England.

Twenty-four horses were shown lots of photos of people's faces. Some of the people were angry. Others were smiling and looked happy.

When the horses saw the angry-face people, their heart rates went up, just like it would if they thought there was danger.

When they saw the smiley faces, this didn't happen. Their heart rates stayed normal.

Then, several hours later, these horses got to meet all the people in the photos for the first time. Incredibly,

One reason horses live in herds is to protect mothers and foals.

they all remembered all the people AND they remembered what mood those people were in, either angry or happy. They were wary of the angry people and wanted to meet the happy people.

Not only do horses recognize people, we now have proof that they recognize human emotions! Dogs are the only other animal proven to have these surprising abilities.

Mama knows best

Horses, like many creatures and people, live in a hierarchy. Hierarchy just means how everyone figures out who is the boss and who better do what they're told.

Every horse family group, or herd, has a lead mare. She is responsible for leading the herd to clean drinking water, safe food and shelter. She usually has a mare assistant who helps her keep the group together and makes the rowdier herd members (these are usually the young stallions) behave themselves.

It's the lead stallion who is the Head of Security. When a herd travels, he stays behind the group to make sure there are no stragglers and everyone is safe.

As they age, the lead mare and lead stallion retire, leaving their jobs to herd members that are younger and stronger.

Horses with jobs

In all the thousands of years horses and people have lived together, the horses have held jobs, as they still do.

In the ancient world, horses carried riders into battle, pulled their chariots and wagons and carried their loads. Some people, who still prefer to live in the old ways, such as Old Order Mennonites and Amish, still use horses and buggies for their transportation.

Here are more jobs horses do today:

They help do farm work, pulling loaded wagons or dragging ploughs through fields.

An Old Order Mennonite family with the working horse that pulls their carriage.

They help cowboys round up cattle on the plains and hills, places where there are no roads.

Horses are used in the forestry industry, helping skid out logs from the forest in winter.

Horses serve in police work, particularly in patrol duties and crowd control.

Park rangers use horses and so do game wardens on patrols because horses are less damaging to the environment than cars or trucks.

Horses are used in search and rescue, able to take their riders into the forest or dense bush where no road vehicles can go to search for hikers or others who are lost.

Horses can be service animals for people with disabilities, helping them strengthen their balance and coordination and increasing their self-confidence.

Horses can be companion animals to assist people with mental illnesses such as anxiety and depression.

Horses entertain, as athletes in racing and show competitions and as actors in movies and TV shows.

People who study human behaviour have discovered that when people in prison are allowed to work with horses, it not only improves the prisoners' behaviour, it makes them less likely to commit crimes after they are released from prison!

Horses are measured in hands

Horses are always measured from the ground to their withers. Withers is the name for the tallest point of their body when they are grazing with their head just above the grass.

Throughout the English-speaking world, horses are measured in hands and inches. A hand is 4 inches (or 102 centimetres). It's called a "hand" because it's the same as the width of an average man's hand.

The first number is full hands, then there is a point, and the next number means plus some inches. So, for example, a horse could be 16.2 hh, or hands high. This means they are 16 hands plus 2 inches tall or 66 inches tall or just over 167 centimetres tall.

This modern shire horse lives in England.

How big are horses?

The average-sized riding horse weighs about 500 kilograms, or 1,100 pounds. They are usually about 15 hands tall. But in the past, and still today, there are horses that are much larger than that.

The Cold Bloods are always the largest horses. The tallest and heaviest horse ever since people started noticing this and writing it down was Mammoth, a Shire Horse who was born in 1846. Mammoth lived in Bedfordshire, England. He was 21.2 ¼ hands tall and weighed 1,524 kilograms or 3,360 pounds.

Since Mammoth's time, there have been other very large horses, including Big Jake, who was born as a large foal in Nebraska 2001. Both his parents were normal-sized Belgians. Big Jake grew up to be 20.2 ¾ hands and weighed 2,600 pounds or 1,179 kilograms as an adult. Big Jake was a big eater. He munched through an entire bale of hay plus two or three buckets of grain every day.

He was so big that his stall needed to be twice as big as a regular horse stall. When he travelled to compete in draft horse competitions, he had to go in a semi-trailer. He was too large to fit in a horse trailer. When travelling got too hard for Big Jake, he retired in 2013.

Sadly, after many years of fame as the largest living horse in the world, Jake died in June 2021 at his home in Wisconsin. He was 20 years old.

The smallest horse in the world

Miniature horses are always small, bred for little children to ride or as pets. They are true horses, not ponies. They look and act just like larger horses, except they're small.

The very smallest miniature horse ever was Thumbelina. She was a miniature horse and also a dwarf. She grew up to be only 4.1 hands tall. As an adult, she weighed just 26 kilograms, or 57 pounds. She was so short that the top of her head barely reached her owner's knees when he stood next to her.

Born in 2001, Thumbelina lived on a farm with other miniature horses in Missouri. She held the Guinness World Record as the world's smallest horse until she died in 2018.

All grown up

Even though some horses race when they are just two years old, horses' muscles and bones don't reach their adult strength and sizes until they are five to six years old.

The larger a horse is, the longer it takes to finish growing. The Cold Bloods - Percherons, Belgians, Shire Horses, Clydesdales and many breeds of draft horses, always take the longest to reach their adult size and strength.

How strong are horses?

Before there were cars and trucks, trains, airplanes or space ships, humans basically had only three ways to get around. They could walk or run where they needed to go. Or use a boat. Or rely on horses to get to where they wanted to be.

A healthy adult horse is much stronger than a healthy adult human. The horse can safely carry 300 to 400 pounds on their back. That's 136 to 181 kilograms. They can also pull a load that is three times their own weight.

Horses are so strong, humans called this power to work "horsepower." Today, one horsepower is the strength it takes to move 550 pounds one foot in one second. That's the same as moving 249.4 kilograms 30.6 centimetres in one second.

One horsepower is about the strength of a horse that works all day, averaged over that entire day. But if the same horse only has to do the task one time, he or she can produce 15 horsepower of strength.

Belgians

Medieval war horses had to be strong. They carried not just their rider, but also his full suit of armour. Belgians are the draft horse that is probably closest to those war horses of long ago. They're also the strongest breed today.

A Belgian can pull up to 3,628 kilograms, or 8,000 pounds of weight. Originally a farm horse, Belgians have been used in forestry, but today are better known for showing their incredible strength in pulling contests. Slimmer and sleeker than the other working horse breeds, they are also used in some equestrian (that means horse riding) events such as dressage.

Belgians don't much care for stables or having their own stalls. They're happy to live outside all year long.

Horse Fun Fact:

There are about 9 million horses in the United States but less than 1 million in United Kingdom.

Horse Fun Fact:

Horses take short naps standing up but must lie down for deep sleep.

You don't want to get bitten by these big teeth!

Horse bites

Something you want to avoid is getting nipped by a horse. That's because their bite force is more than twice as bad as getting bitten by, say, your little brother.

But horses' bites look wimpy compared to some of the world's fiercest biters!

Here's the biting leader board, measured in psi, which means pounds per square inch:

- 4,000 Great White Shark
- 3,700 Saltwater Crocodiles
- 2,980 American Crocodiles
- 1,800 Hippopotamus
- 1,500 Jaguars
- 1,300 Gorillas
- 1,200 Polar Bears
- 1,050 Bengal Tigers
- 500 Horses
- 200 Human bite force

Sounds like if you had a biting cage match the sharks would win! But not if they were up against the greatest biter of all time. That would be Tyrannosaurus Rex whose impressive chompers could bite you with 431,342 psi. Aren't you glad you don't have one of them as a pet?

Thoroughbreds

Thoroughbreds are bred to be spirited and fast. They're a tall horse, usually closer to 17 hands than 15. Besides racing, they're also very good at jumping, polo and dressage because they're not just speedy

Thoroughbreds racing. Though that's what they're known for, this breed is also a good riding horse for intermediate or advanced riders.

horses, they're also good at agility. This means they can change directions quickly.

All of the English mares who had the first Thoroughbred foals belonged to English Kings. This is why the mothers of this breed are known as the Royal Mares. They were owned by James I and Charles I of Great Britain.

Their sires were three breeds of fast horses from the Middle East. One of these sires, now called the Darley Arabian, is the ancestor sire of almost every Thoroughbred alive today.

How fast are horses?

Who, and what breed, is the fastest horse? There are two answers to this question, depending on if you want to know about the fastest sprinting horse or the fastest horse in a full race.

Sprinting is running very hard and fast for a short distance.

Races are longer distances.

The winner in the sprinting race would be a Thoroughbred. A filly named Winning Brew holds the record for fastest sprint. She was clocked going 43.97 miles per hour. That's 70.76 kilometres per hour. Compare that to what an average riding horse can do, which is about 27 miles per hour, or 43.45 kilometres per hour.

So, what about the longer race? That record isn't held by a Thoroughbred, but by a Quarter Horse called A Long Goodbye. In 2005, A Long Goodbye galloped at 55 miles per hour, or 88.5 kilometres per hour, the fastest any horse has ever run.

How old do horses get?

The normal lifetime of a horse is between 25 and 30 years, but some horses can live longer than this. Much longer, for Old Billy, a horse born in Lancashire, England in 1760. He spent a long working life dragging barges loaded with goods. Barges were long, flat boats on the canals. They had no engines, because engines hadn't been invented yet. Instead, horses on the shore dragged these boats along, using long ropes.

Old Billy the Canal Horse died in 1822, aged 62. He was a celebrity later in his life and even after he died. You can still see his skull on display in England at the Manchester Museum.

A purebred isn't the same as a thoroughbred

A Thoroughbred is a breed of horse. Purebred means a horse is totally one breed. Both their parents and all their grandparents were the same breed. Horses can also be mixed breeds.

Each purebred breed has their own breed registry. The breed registries are the ones who say what that breed needs to look like, coat colours, and their personality in order for a new foal to be registered with them as a purebred.

There are no wild horses

Maybe you've heard about an island conservation area or park you can visit to see wild horses. They live in herds and enjoy life with no job to do except show up to entertain visitors.

But are these horses you're going to see really, truly wild? Probably not. The reason is that they are actually feral horses. Feral means they – or maybe their parents or grandparents or great-grandparents –

Feral horses enjoy a wild life, but usually live shorter lives than horses that live with people.

were tame, but they escaped or got loose. There are many animals in the world this is true for. Wild dogs, wild cats, even wild budgies that used to be pets but got loose and now live a wild, or sort-of-wild, life. They're not wild. They're all feral animals.

So are the Mustangs of the American West, the Brumbies of Australia, the Chincoteague Ponies of Virginia and Maryland in the U.S. and the Sable Island Ponies of Nova Scotia in Canada.

It's exciting to think that somewhere in the world, in some very remote place, there could still be truly wild horses running free, but this is fiction, not a fact. There are no truly wild horses left in the world.

There are no albino horses

There are horses with a white coat and pale pink skin, but no horse has pink eyes. There are no albino horses.

Albino means they have no melanin in their skin or eyes. It is melanin that gives skin, or eyes, their colours. Albinos have pale or white skin and pink eyes. Being albino can happen in animals and also in people.

Being an albino is inherited. This means it's something you get from your parents. If you're born albino, you don't grow out of it. It's very rare.

People or animals who are albinos have very sensitive skin and usually have trouble seeing, or they might be blind. Otherwise, they're just as healthy as any other animal or person.

But none of them are horses. The reason is if a horse is accidentally albino, it won't live long enough to be born.

Lightning fast reflexes

If something frightened you and you had to move fast to defend yourself, how long do you think it would take you to react?

The answer is 1.6 seconds, according to scientists who have studied this. Sounds pretty fast, doesn't it?

But any horse would leave your reaction time in the dust! If horses suddenly find they either need to fight or run away, they do it in just a third of a second!

A very young foal, resting in her field. She can smell her mother as well as hear her, so isn't afraid of getting lost.

That's five times faster than any human could react. In a dangerous situation, your horse would understand and react while you, with slower human reflexes, were just noticing the situation!

Horse ages

We sometimes refer to people only by their age group. Children are 12 years old or younger. Teens are age 13 to 19. Everyone is an adult after that.

There are also age groups for horses.

A Foal is less than one year old.

A Yearling is 1 to 2 years old.

A Colt is a young male horse, under age four or, in the United Kingdom (UK), under age 5.

A Filly is a young female horse under age four or, in the UK, under age 5.

A Stallion is an adult male age 4 or older, or age 5 or older in the UK.

A Gelding is an adult male horse who isn't able to make a female horse, called a mare, pregnant.

A Mare is an adult female age 4 or older, or older than 5 in the UK.

A Senior is a Stallion, Gelding or Mare who is 20 years old or older and is retired.

Foal facts

Foals, like human babies, are usually born at night.

A new foal weighs about 50 pounds.

Some foals are born bow-legged. In horses, this is called being a windswept foal. It happens when a larger foal is born to a small mare. Within a few days, as their legs become stronger, their legs usually straighten up.

Horses' legs are nearly as long when they're born as they will be when they're adults. Breeders and owners can do a string test on a new foal and know how big that foal will be when they're an adult. It's a simple

Foals have a belly button.

test and surprisingly accurate. Here's how to do it. Hold a piece of string between the centre of one knee in one hand and the top of the hoof in your other hand. Then measure how long that is. If it's 15 inches, this foal will grow up to be a 15 hh adult.

Foals can stand up just minutes after they're born. By 120 minutes (or two hours) after their birth, they can walk. They know how to gallop before they're a full day old.

Horse birthdays

Here is a strange fact about horse birthdays. No matter what date a Thoroughbred racehorse is born, officially their birthday is January 1 of their birth year in the Northern Hemisphere. In the Southern

A Standardbred mare and her twins. Mares commonly have as many as 13 foals in their lifetime.

Hemisphere, the official horse birthday is August 1 of their year.

The Kentucky Derby and the Preakness are two famous horse races. Only three-year-old horses are eligible to compete in these races, even though race horses usually run faster when they are older than three.

In endurance, or long-distance races, this odd birthday fact isn't true. In long races, the horse's true age, using their real birthday, is the rule for what ages the horses can be to compete.

Horse Fun Fact:

Horses can only breathe through their nose.

Horse twins

It's rare for a mare to have twins, and extremely rare for a mare to have triplets, but it does sometimes happen. The reason is that there simply isn't enough space for two babies, or three, to grow inside their mother.

Humans mothers are 30 times more likely to have twins than mares are.

There are some breeds that are a bit more likely to have twins than the others. These are Thoroughbreds, Standardbreds and some of the other Warm Bloods.

It's incredibly rare for a horse to have triplets. It happens just once for every 300,000 births.

Capture that goat!

Here's a crazy horse sport with goats where you really don't want to be the goat!

It's call Buzkashi, a team game played on horseback that is popular in Central Asia. Each team tries to capture the body of a dead goat from the other team and get that goat into the other team's goal to earn points.

It's a bit like hockey, without the sticks but one big, dead and smelly puck.

Horse Fun Fact:

When a horse's ears are turned to the side and her head is lowered, it's a sign that she's happy.

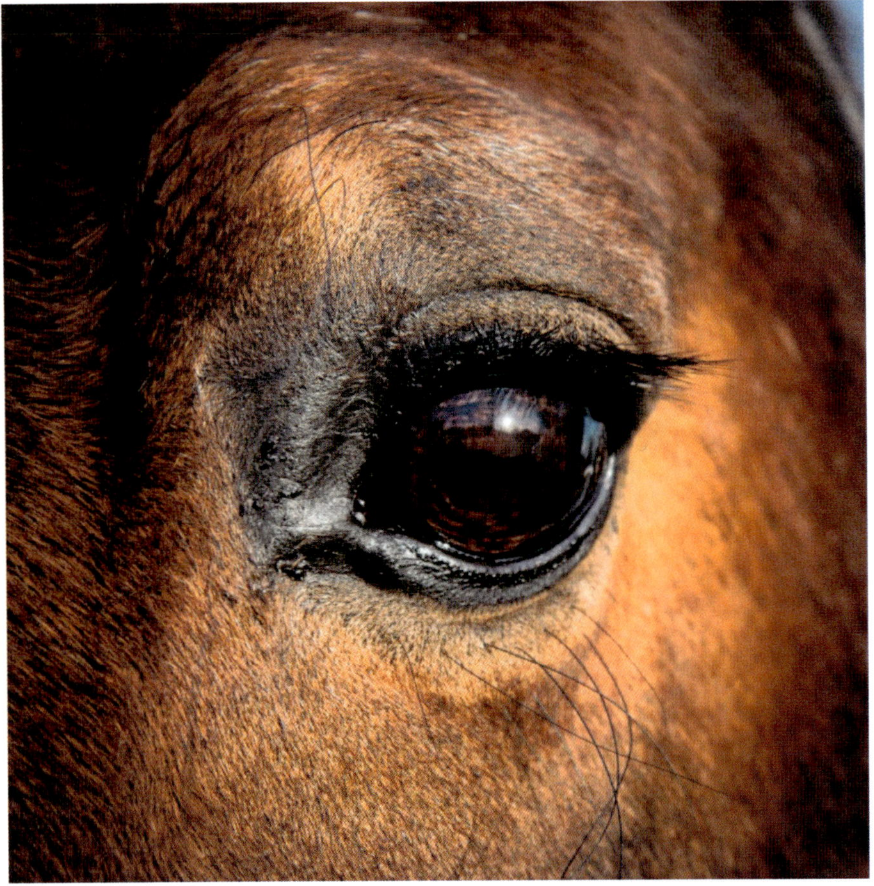

Horses' eyes are on the sides of their heads, changing the way they see their world.

Predator or prey? Look at my eyes and you'll know!

You can always tell if an animal is a predator animal or a prey animal by looking at their eyes.

It's not about how they see, or what they see. It's about where their eyes are placed on their heads.

If their eyes are on the sides of their heads, they're prey. If their eyes look forward, and they have a flat face, they're a predator.

Predators need to be able to look straight ahead. This allows them to see the creatures they hunt. To survive, prey must be able to look in all directions to spot danger. Prey usually are good at seeing things close up but don't have very good distance vision. They need to spot things that are the immediate danger.

Looking two ways at once!

With eyes on the sides of their heads, horses can see things in front of them, beside them and almost all the way behind them. They can't see directly behind their own head, so they can't see a rider on their back. They also can't see right under their own nose!

Horses are able to see two completely different views at one time; one with each eye. Each eye sends its own message to their brain. That's completely different than the way human eyes work. Our eyes see two slightly different images, but then our brains combine those two into one image.

This is how we understand what we are looking at and also how far away it is from us. This helps us focus and also gives us what's called depth perception. Depth perception is being able to see the width, length and depth of objects.

Horses see all around themselves. They need to concentrate to be able to focus on just one thing. They are not very good at depth perception, which means they aren't very good at judging how far away something is from themselves.

Horses are better than we are at detecting even the slightest thing moving from a distance. They aren't as good as people are at seeing details in things that are close to them.

More about horses' eyes

Like many animals, horses have better vision at night than people do.

They can see in colour, but not like we do. Most people can see three colours (yellow, blue and red) from which all the other colours are made. This is called trichromatic vision.

Horses have dichromatic vision. They can only see two colours. These are blue and yellow, plus the combination of those colours to make green. They can't tell the difference between red and green.

Listening two ways at once!

Humans have just two muscles in their ears, which is why most of us can't move our ears around the way a horse can. Horses have ten muscles in each ear. This allows them to move their ears to gather sounds, like satellite dishes.

If you want to know what a horse is thinking right now, look at where their ears are pointing. If their

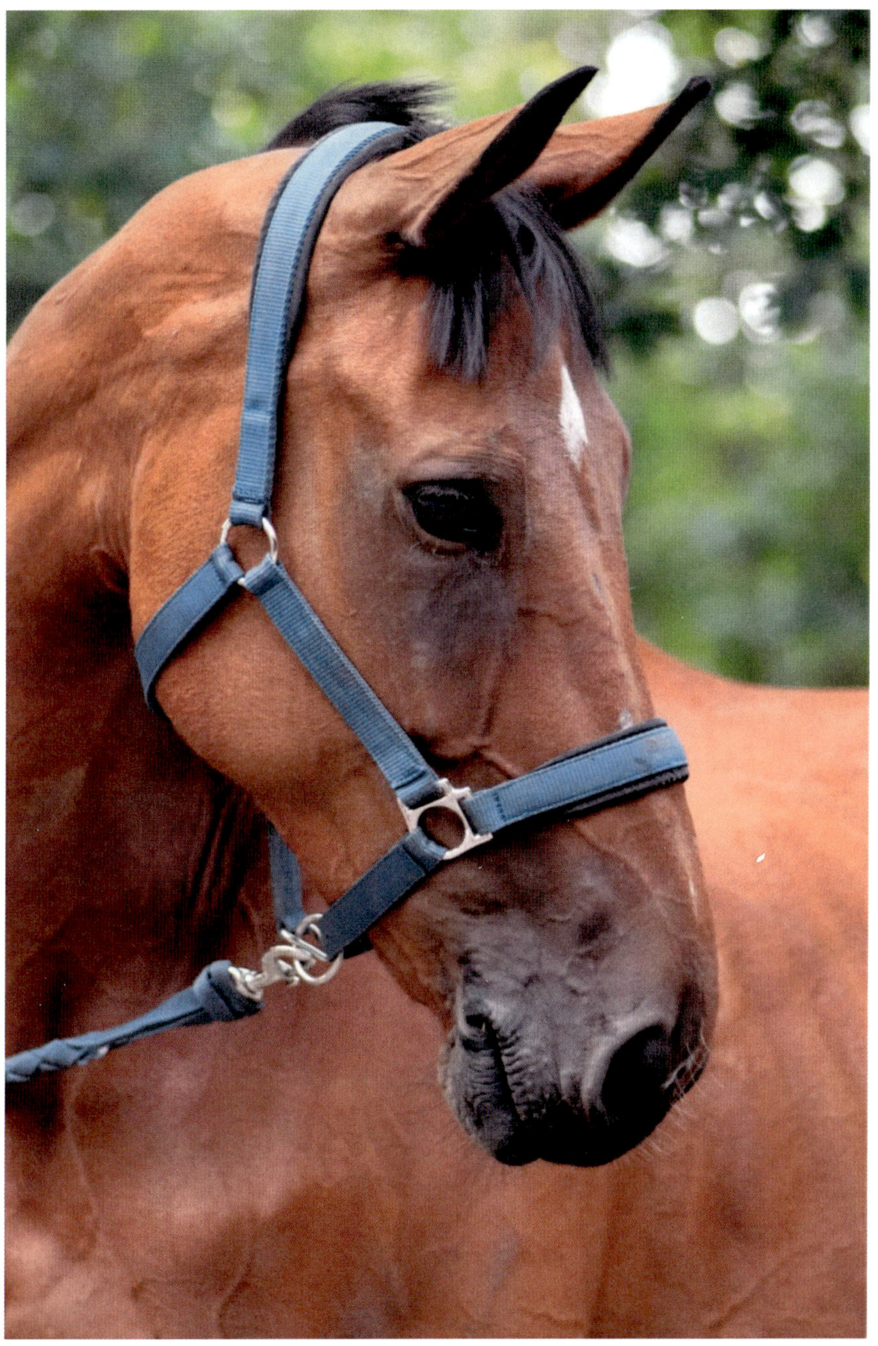

Horses' ears always point towards what they're interested in right now.

ears are just gently flopped to the side, they are relaxed and happy and not listening to anything right now except the rest of the herd.

Mouth full of teeth

Horses have most of their teeth in the front of their mouth. Stallions and Geldings have four more teeth than Mares. All horses can have four very small teeth in the backs of their mouths. These are called wolf teeth. Sometimes they're removed to make the bit fit properly in their mouths.

Humans get just two sets of teeth. These are baby teeth and the final set of teeth that start to grow in when you're around age 8. Horses continually wear down their teeth and continually get new ones growing in. Their teeth also change as they get older. This is why looking in their mouths is one way to know how old a horse is.

Big-hearted horses

Horses have large lungs, allowing them to take in more air. They also have large hearts. HUGE hearts!

The average adult horse has a heart that is between nine and ten pounds or four to four and a half kilograms. That's more than ten times as big as an adult human heart.

Racehorses are even more big-hearted than their riding-horse cousins. Secretariat lived from 1970 to 1989 and won more than $1.3 million in racing prizes,

A farrier cleans a horses' hooves, trims them and fits the shoes.

including winning the Triple Crown in 1983. His heart weighed twice as much as an average horse.

How big is your favourite horse's heart? Here's an easy way to tell. A horse's heart is usually about one percent of his or her body weight.

Some horses wear shoes

Horses' hooves are made out of the same material that makes fingernails in humans. Just like our fingernails, their hooves grow constantly. In one month, human fingernails grow about 3.47 millimetres, or .135 of an inch. So it would take about two and a half years to grow your fingernails 1 inch beyond the ends of your fingers.

A horse's hooves grow much faster; 1.4 inches per month, about ten times as fast as human fingernails grow. A horse could grow an entire new hoof in a year.

When horses were wild, their hooves naturally wore down with all the running they did. Modern horses don't have big spaces to run in. This is why they need their hooves trimmed regularly. A farrier is the specialist who trims hooves properly and fits horse shoes. Horses need to see their farrier about every six weeks.

Kicking horses

If you get kicked by a horse, it's going to hurt! But did you know that a horse kick is powerful enough to kill a person? It's true.

Kicking to kill isn't what the horse meant to do. Well-trained horses just about never kick. Well-trained horse owners know their horse well enough to know when he or she is about to kick.

An average adult horse's kicking force is 2,000 psi. Psi means pounds force per square inch. The speed of a horse kick has been clocked at an average of 200 miles per hour, or 322 kilometres per hour.

Getting kicked with 2,000 psi is the same as being hit by a car that's going 20 miles per hour or 32 kilometres per hour.

A horse kick is pretty impressive, but it's not the animal wallop winner. In psi, here's the force of:

A T-Rex bite - 431,000

A major league baseball player's swing, hitting the ball - 8,314

A crocodile bite - 5,000

A professional golfer's swing, hitting the ball - 4,000

A great white shark bite - 3,800

And all of these are going to come in behind the horse kick, in the psi stakes: hippo bite, a heavyweight boxer's punch, or a bite by a gorilla, lion, grizzly bear or polar bear.

Red ribbon tails

When you go to a horse show or competition, you might notice that some owners tie a bright red ribbon on their horses' tails. They don't do this just for pretty. The red ribbon is there to warn other people that this horse is a kicker, and to stay well back.

Horses can't see red and aren't likely to take much notice of ribbons, unless they have to wear them themselves, which they might object to.

Can horses laugh?

Horse laugh is a saying that people might use when someone has a really loud, annoying way of laughing. That someone would be human, because horses can't

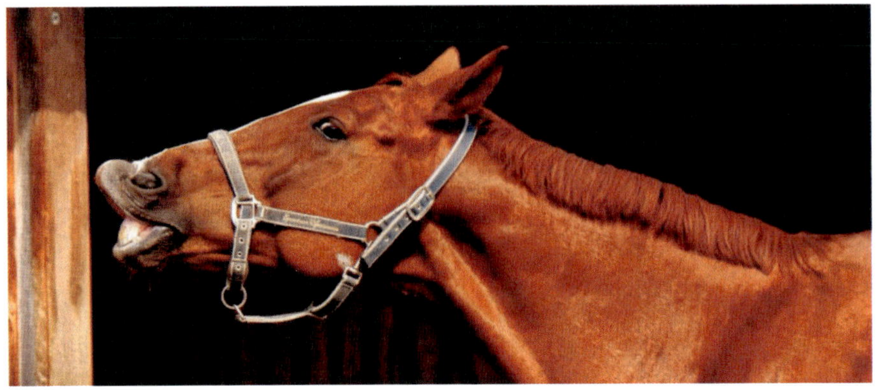

This horse is getting a good sniff of something interesting. It might be a nearby mare he'd like to get to know.

laugh. Like all animals, they don't have a sense of humour. They don't understand jokes.

But horses do something that looks just like they're laughing. They aren't, so what is it they're really doing?

The answer is they're getting an even better sniff of the air for any interesting aromas around. They lift their head up high and peel back their top lip to get more air to their Jacobson's Organ. It is just above the roof of their mouth. This organ works like a second smelling system, along with their nose.

Stallions use it to sniff for mares who might be interested in mating. Doing this is called the Flehman Response. All horses do it, but males, even very young colts, do it more often.

Horses like sweet or salty foods. Their favourite treat is carrots.

Can horses taste their food?

If someone told you that you eat like a horse, they wouldn't mean that you like to eat grass! "Eat like a horse" is an expression that means eating a LOT. And just about never stopping.

That's exactly what horses do. They spend most of the time they're awake eating. They eat during the day and at night. An average horse eats 15 to 24 pounds or 7 to 11 kilograms of food in every 24-hour period of time.

Horses are much better at tasting their food than people are. That's because people have about 8,000

The main food for modern horses is fresh grass or hay. Their ancient ancestors enjoyed a different menu.

taste buds on our tongues, but horses have 25,000 taste sensors!

Horses like things that taste sweet, like fresh grass and carrots. They also enjoy salty tasting things, but won't eat something that is sour or bitter.

Not liking bitter-tasting foods protects them from eating plants that are poisonous for them.

Horses are picky about their food and their water. If anything smells a bit odd, they won't go near it, even when they're hungry or thirsty.

These foods are unhealthy for horses: meat, bread, cake, human salty snacks like chips, chocolate, turnips, cabbages, kale, broccoli, Brussels sprouts, potatoes and tomatoes.

Did ancient horses eat like modern horses do?

Throughout their long history, horses have always been herbivores. This means they eat plants or things plants make, like seeds. For the first 35 million years horses were on earth they were much smaller than horses are today. They were probably about as big as a Labrador retriever dog.

All of these ancient wild horses ate grass, when they could find it, but also needed to eat shrubs, trees, other plants and bushes. They had to do this to get all the nutrients they needed.

Scientists say that horses developed a liking for sweets because eating sugary foods puts on fat. Having some extra fat would help them get through times when there was less food around, like in winter.

Modern horses graze on fresh grass, but they also eat hay, grains and get supplements in their horse feed.

Horses are touchy!

Horses are very sensitive to being touched, especially around their eyes, ears and on their soft noses.

Their entire body is as sensitive as your fingertips!

Competing in a barrel race, something you'll see if you go to a rodeo.

When you are riding, they can feel even the slightest movement or shift in your weight. Touch is a signal to them, just like words are to you.

American Quarter Horse

Intelligent, gentle, and usually not much bigger than pony-sized, American Quarter Horses are the most popular breed in the United States. They have been bred to be easy to handle for young and adult riders, including beginners.

This breed was created back in the 1500s when ranch owners imported Thoroughbred stallions from Europe and bred them with their ranch horse mares.

Muscular and stocky, American Quarter Horses got their name not because they are a quarter of the size of most horses, but because of their ability to win short quarter mile or .4 kilometre races.

Today, they are most often used for Western riding and competing in rodeos.

Why do horses like to roll around on the ground?

When you see a horse on his or her back, legs waving in the air, it looks kind of silly. So why do they do it?

Is it because they have an itchy back? Or maybe just because they feel like it? Maybe. But here are some other reasons horses roll around on the ground:

To dry their coat after it rains.

To get rid of flies.

To mark their territory.

Horses with long memories

If someone said you've got a memory like a horse, would that be a good thing? Absolutely! Horses have very good memories, and not just for the places that have good food, fresh water or shelter.

Horses remember people by their smell, their tone of voice, but also by their faces. Even though they don't use words to communicate, they do use sounds. They

Healthy young horse teeth.

remember sounds and voices, both ones they like and ones they don't.

A hundred years ago and more, most things were delivered by horse and wagon. One of these things was milk, which came in bottles the milkman brought to your front door every morning. The milkman's horses, usually looking sporty in straw hats, remembered their route and always knew exactly which houses to stop at.

Like all horses, they picked up their pace each day on their milk run when they'd turned back towards their own homes.

Do horses have small brains?

An adult horse's brain weighs about 22 ounces or 623.6 grams. That's about half as big as an adult human's brain weighs.

Horses' brains take up less space in their heads than their teeth do.

Even though it might seem that horses wouldn't be very smart, given their larger bodies but smaller brains compared to people, this isn't true. Horses are intelligent and can do some surprising things.

Horse Fun Fact:

Horses first evolved about 55 million years ago. That was long before we did. The first human ancestors appeared on earth about five or six million years ago.

Arabians are known for being smart, spirited and fast.

Are horses smart?

Yes. Horses are naturally curious and will investigate things they haven't seen before. When they can't solve a problem, they figure out a way to get their humans to solve it for them.

All horses can learn simple things, but two breeds are known for being especially clever. These are Thoroughbreds and Arabians. Standardbreds can also be pretty smart.

All horses have the ability to know what other horses are thinking. They do this by watching where others in their herds are looking, and what direction their ears are turned in.

Back in 1904, Beautiful Jim Key was a hit at the St. Louis World's Fair in the United States for his skills in reading, spelling, and doing simple math problems with numbers under 30. Newspapers of that time reported that Beautiful Jim Key could cite verses in The Bible that mention horses.

Here's another smart horse story. Lucas, a retired racehorse, had a second career demonstrating his skills identifying letters, numbers, shapes and even colours! In 2010, he won the Guinness World Records title for most numbers identified correctly by a horse in one minute. Clever Lucas could recognize 19 numbers, which makes him a horse celebrity!

Who's smarter, horses or dogs?

The answer is that they're both smart, in different ways. Horses can learn things faster than dogs. Dogs are better at solving problems than horses.

Horses don't like windy weather

Horses dislike wind for three reasons.

1. Wind makes them worried and confused. It moves things around more. Horses are always hyper aware of where they are and what else is around them. As prey animals, they're always ready to rush away from danger. Things moving suddenly will scare them. So do unfamiliar sounds, because it might mean a hidden enemy, like a wolf, or maybe a lion, is stalking them.

2. Wind carries scents from further away. This means there are more scents to sniff and figure out what they are and if they're dangerous.
3. Wind carries sounds from further away than they're used to. This puts them on high alert for dangers that could be so far away it means nothing to their safety in their own field.

More things horses really don't like

Horses are individuals. They each have their likes and dislikes, just like people do. But there are things just about every horse really doesn't like. Do any of these things with your horse and they are going to be doing some serious tail swishing! If you really annoy them and just don't listen to what they're trying to tell you, watch out!

What horses just hate:

1. Any sudden or loud noise, like people shouting. They like quiet, calm voices.
2. Tack that doesn't fit. Tack is all the things you use to ride a horse, such as the saddle, halter and bridle. Worn out or loose tack can cause them to be sore or injured.
3. Shoes that don't fit. It hurts them to walk and can injure them.
4. Poor riders. They don't like having people on their backs who just don't know what they're doing.

5. People who don't understand horses.
6. Being left in their stall too much. They get bored. Unless they're sick, they'd always rather be running around outside with their herd.
7. Having no horse friends. As a herd animal, they feel happy, comforted and protected by their herd or nervous, lonely and scared with no mates. To a horse, a herd-mate can be a horse, pony, donkey or even a goat. Horses are particularly happy with a donkey friend.
8. People who are impatient or unkind. Just like people, horses learn best and are happiest when they are treated with patience and kindness.

Sounds horses make and what they mean

Nicker Is a soft sound horses use to greet each other or people they like.

Squeal is what horses do when they distrust something. The louder the squeal, the more worried your horse is.

Whinny is a loud sound that means "Where are you?" to another horse who's lost, or it can be a distress signal to the herd. Neighing is another word for whinnying.

Snort is another loud sound and a way that herds communicate to be sure everyone hears. It means fear or danger.

Horses will cross streams, and even swim, when they have to. Most horses don't enjoy swimming.

Clacking is a noise young horses make by clicking their teeth. They do it to tell the older members of their herd that they're just little and to please not hurt them. They usually stop clacking when they're two to three years old.

Horses and water

Horses don't drink water like we do. They also don't lap up water like a cat or dog. Instead, they're able to shape their lips like a straw and use suction to get their drink. It's just like you using a straw.

Horses drink between 10 and 25 US gallons of water per day. That's about 38 to 95 litres – every day!

Horses find donkeys to be loyal and calming friends.

They can swim and they're good at it, but feral horses usually don't swim by choice. To them, a river or a lake is a barrier between where they are now and where to want to go.

Domesticated horses (that's the ones that live with people), are usually worried about water at first, but most horses can learn to enjoy swimming. When they do get the opportunity, they can become very good swimmers.

Their strength, big hearts and large lungs give them endurance and a natural ability to float. Like dogs, horses have an instinct to paddle with their legs.

Horse friends

If you go to a horse race, you might see that the racehorses are walked out to the starting gate with a companion horse.

Racehorses have another horse with them before the race to help them ignore all the crowd noises, stay calm and be as relaxed as possible. The companion horse is called a pony horse, even though it's usually a horse, not a pony. This is just the name. The Pony Horse is an important member of their racing team, helping racehorses focus on winning!

Do horses know their own names?

Some horse owners say that no horse knows their own name. Others strongly disagree. So who's right?

Horses that spend lots of time with one owner can learn their own name, as well as other words, perhaps as many as the average two-year-old child. It could be that it isn't the word itself they've learnt, but the sound and tone of voice is what they understand. This is also true for commands, like "Walk!" or "Whoa!" When you always use the same tone of voice, and are

Horses would always rather be outside running, playing, resting and being a member of their own herd.

patient and gentle in your teaching, horses learn what these sounds mean.

Strange sleepers

Horses have two ways of sleeping. They take short naps all day long, standing up. They also have to lie down to sleep for a few hours every day, or night. Very young horses and seniors tend to sleep for longer each day than adults.

To sleep standing up, they lock their legs and doze. Any sudden noise will wake them up. If they are outside, while some of the herd are sleeping, others will stay awake, standing guard.

A horse that lives alone, with no herd, is a worried horse. They can't sleep well because their instinct is to only sleep when there's another horse watching out for danger.

Horses have to have some lying down sleep every day in order to get deep sleep. A horse that is always in a stall that is too small for them to be able to lie down will suffer, just as humans do when they don't get enough sleep.

Do horses like to play?

Yes, Horses love play fighting. They will run and leap, kick and nip each other. It might look like fighting, but it's not. They'll play fight for a while, take a break and then go back at it. As long as nobody gets hurt, they're having a great time. Just like you, play wrestling with other kids when you were younger.

But all this horsey play fighting isn't just for the fun. They're also figuring out who is stronger, and so has a higher rank in their herd hierarchy.

Horse fights

As a prey animal, horses would almost always rather run than fight. When that is impossible or when their foal is threatened, they will stand and fight.

Horse friends groom each other and stand back to front, swishing their tails, to protect each other from flies.

Stallions also fight to compete for mares in mating season.

Ain't Misbehaving!

When people are mistreated, they tend to react. So do horses.

A horse that doesn't get to be part of a herd, is left for long periods without any companionship in their stall or shed, or doesn't get enough exercise and attention is going to show their resentment.

Some of the signs of an unhappy horse are wood chewing, wall kicking, rocking back and forth and trying to bite anyone who gets close.

Horse Fun Fact:

Just like your fingernails and toenails, horses' hooves keep growing for all of their lives.

A horse that likes you wants to be with you.

Does your horse like you?

One easy way to tell your horse likes you is the answer to this question: "Do they follow you around?"

Horses only follow each other, or people, who they count as friends. Here are some other ways horses show they like you:

- They whinny or nicker to you to say "Hello."
- They rest their head on your shoulder.
- They nudge you gently.
- They breathe a puff of air in your face.
- They follow your commands.

Can a horse get sunburn?

Yes, some horses can get sunburn, which is why they always need a sheltered place in their field. Horses that have pink skin, which is usual for horses that are gray or white, can get sunburn. So can horses that have pink or white skin on their noses.

War horses

Poison gas was a new weapon in World War I. It happened in 1914 to 1919 in Europe, Africa and involved most of the countries of the world. To protect themselves, warriors wore gas masks, and so did their horses, donkeys, mules and dogs.

Horses have can smell more, from further away, than people can.

Horse gas masks were first developed by the Germans. They also were the first to make and put gas masks on their dogs on the battlefields.

Super sniffers!

Horses can smell things better than people can, but not nearly as good as any dog can. They use smell to identify each other. Every foal and his or her mother know each other's smell at a foal's birth.

What kind of music do horses like?

Some horses seem to like country, easy listening or classical music, but they'd rather not have to listen to jazz or rock music. That's what one study in England found, in 2013.

Another study, in Australia, found that racehorses who have to listen to talk radio get more gastric ulcers that their mates listening to just music. Gastric ulcers are sores in your stomach that are painful. They're mainly caused by stress. Many animals and also people can get ulcers.

The healthiest horses, it turns out, enjoy the peace and quiet of no radio and no music at all.

Horses can't burp or throw up

Ancient horse ancestors, the horses of millions of years ago, probably were able to throw up. They could probably also burp, when they needed to. But modern horses have lost this ability because when food or water goes down their esophagus and into their stomach, a valve closes. This means what goes down can't ever come back up again.

Horses can read human emotions

Horses can recognize human feelings and emotions. They also have very long memories. They do remember the angry or mean-spirited person they

Horses can sense what you're feeling, even when you're riding and they can't see you. This girl is riding bareback, without a saddle.

met, or the sweet and kind person by what mood that person was in the last time they saw them!

It seems that in the thousands of years that horses and people have lived together and worked together, horses have learned how to read people's faces and body language, as well as understand the tone of voice they use. The only other animal that can do this is dogs.

Horses are stressed when they see an angry face or hear angry voices. They like calm, quiet voices. Like most people, they're rather avoid dramas.

Horses can recognize themselves in a mirror

Most animals are afraid, or disturbed and perhaps angry when they see their own reflection in glass or a mirror. Some will even try to attack it!

But, amazingly, horses recognize themselves in mirrors, or reflected in calm water. How can they do this? How do they know what they look like, since horses often don't look like their mothers or even like anyone else in the herd? Experts don't have these answers. Yet.

Horses can't do the splits

Even if they really wanted to, no horse can do the splits.

The reason is they have a pelvis that is fixed in place. The pelvis, on a horse or a human, is where their body meets their legs. Humans have a more flexible pelvis, so most people can learn to do the splits.

Are horses afraid of butterflies?

There are animals horses just don't like because they're not sure what that creature is going to do next. This includes birds and butterflies. They aren't afraid of them, they just don't like them.

Another thing that horses find really worrying is any sudden noise, like barking, which is why they don't

Horses see in colour, but not the same way we do.

like dogs. Or cats.

While they can be curious about snakes, they will almost always run away if that snake moves or makes a sound, like a rattle-snake.

Are horses afraid of rainbows?

During a parade you might have seen riders trying to control their horses who shy away or try to prance sideways when they come to a rainbow crossing on the street. The reason is that horses can see colour, but they see it the same way that people who have red-green colour blindness do. This means they can see blue, green or yellow as well as gray as these colours truly are, but red or orange looks the same as green, or perhaps it looks like brown or gray.

Also, horses don't like things they aren't already familiar with. To them, a paved road shouldn't suddenly have blue, yellow, green and gray stripes. It just seems wrong to them. To a horse, anything that seems wrong might be dangerous. If so, to their way of thinking, it's better to avoid it.

Are horses afraid of plastic bags?

Plastic food store bags might have been banned where you live, or perhaps not yet. They're useful, but a threat to the environment. They turn up everywhere as litter, including being caught in tree branches, where they can flutter and make strange noises if there's a breeze.

Over millions of years, horses have learned to be wary of any sudden, strange noise. That's what the rattle of a plastic bag is to them, making them spook when out riding. It may seem silly to us that a big, strong animal would be afraid of a small plastic bag, but experienced riders know to look out for bags in trees, or anywhere near the trail, particularly on windy days.

Horse gaits

All horses naturally have four ways of moving. These are called gaits. Some breeds naturally have more than four gaits. The four natural gaits all horses are born being able to do are:

When horses gallop, there is a fraction of a second when all four hooves are in the air!

Walk Horses naturally walk at 3 to 5 miles per hour (mph), or 5 to 8 kilometres per hour (kmh).

Trot or Jog This is the clip-clop gait. It's usually 5 to 8 mph or 8 to 13 kmh. Trotting is faster in harness racing. Instead of a trot or jog, some horse breeds have a two-beat gait called a Pace.

Canter or Lope Horses canter at almost 10 to 16.8 mph or 16 to 27 kmh. It's a three-beat gait.

Gallop This is the fastest horse gait, 25 to 30 mph or 40 to 48 kmh. The fastest recorded gallop is almost 44 mph or 70.7 kmh.

Breeds that have additional gaits

Some breeds have developed, or been trained to do, even more than the four basic gaits. The Tennessee Walking Horse has a fancy walk that the breed is known for. Some other special gaits are called the Rack, Running Walk, Tolt and Fox Trot.

Long stride

Horses don't have a collarbone, like people do. Instead, they have a group of muscles, tendons and ligaments to attach their front legs to their shoulders. This allows them to have a much longer reach and stride. They can take much bigger steps, one of the things that allows them to run fast. Having a collarbone would slow them down!

Horses have three eyelids!

Just like humans, horses have upper and lower eyelids. This allows them to blink to clean their eyes or close their eyes to sleep. Their upper eyelid is bigger. It can move more than the lower eyelid. You could think of these upper and lower eyelids as something like window blinds that move down, or up, to cover a window.

Horses also have a third eyelid. This third eyelid doesn't close from the top or the bottom of their eye. Instead, it moves diagonally from the inside of the eye to the other side, something like a curtain closing over

Jumping is a popular event at equestrian competitions.

a window. The purpose of their third eyelids is to protect the corneas of their eyes.

Horses aren't the only animals to have three eyelids. So do polar bears, kangaroos, beavers, seals and some fish, lizards and birds.

Horses are powerful jumpers

Horses' back legs are longer and stronger than their front legs. This means that they can learn to become powerful jumpers. Some horses naturally love jumping.

The Mongol Derby is the world's toughest horse race

Can you imagine a 621 mile, or 1,000 kilometre race across the hills of Mongolia? Riders and their horses have to cross rivers, make their way through marshes, mountain passes and forests and over sand dunes. Every rider is in the saddle for 13 or 14 hours every day for this 10-day race.

Not only do you need to be a very experienced rider to enter The Mongol Derby, you must pay £11,375 to have the honour of being a competitor! That's about $15,000 in American dollars, or $20,500 Australian dollars. And, just to make it even tougher, the horses in this race aren't the racers' own horses. They're semi-feral horses supplied by the race organizers.

Riders must change horses every 40 kilometres, or 25 miles. Riders who push their horses too hard on the trail can be given a time penalty. This race is so challenging that only half the competitors who start the race make it to the finish line most years.

Thanks for reading!

Jacquelyn

Horse Fun Fact:

Horses can smell if there is medicine hidden in their food or water. If so, they won't want it, even when they're hungry or thirsty.

About the Author

Jacquelyn Elnor Johnson started telling stories to entertain her younger sisters, discovering in the telling what it takes to engage your audience! By age 15, she was a correspondent for the local newspaper and had written her first book. She went on to have careers in writing for and editing newspapers and magazines and teaching journalism.

In 2014, she moved with her family to Nova Scotia, drawn by the opportunity to live near the ocean. With the move came a change of focus to creating fun books for kids ages 8 to 12. A life-long pet lover, she is the bestselling author of 13 books about caring for and enjoying pets and animals, including **I Want A Bearded Dragon** and **The Complete Bearded Dragon Care Book.**

In addition to writing practical, helpful and entertaining non-fiction, she writes novels including the Morley Stories series for girls ages 10 to 13.

Find all these books and more at **www.CrimsonHillBooks.com**

PHOTO CREDITS

Thank you to these photo artists:

Shutterstock: Jill Richardson King, Groome, Barbara Fraatz

Pixabay: Ralph Siebeck, Albrecht Fietz, Dendoktoor, Balvda Dariusz, Jessica Rockerman, B. Snuffleupagus, Antonios Ntoumas, M. VanHartesveld0, Arjanne Holsappel, Alexas Fotos, Clarence Alford, Keishpixl, 127071, Ada K., Ruth Archer, Christel Sagniez, Couleur, David Mark, F. Muhammad, Pezibear, Ulrike Leone, The Other Kev, Karsten Paulick, Dreamtemp, Katerina Hartlova, Elmer L. Geissler, T.C. Developer, Carlito Canhadas, Candice, Perlenmuschel,Tomacz Proszek, Kira Hoffmann, Reheij, Rebecca Scholz, Siggy Nowak

Loved all these great facts and photos? Discover MORE about your favourite pets and animals in these books:

- **I Want A Bearded Dragon**
- **I Want A Leopard Gecko**
- **I Want A Kitten**
- **I Want A Puppy**

- **Fun Leopard Gecko and Bearded Dragon Facts for Kids**
- **Fun Reptile Facts for Kids**
- **Fun Dog Facts for Kids**
- **Fun Cat Facts for Kids**
- **Fun Pony Facts for Kids**
- **Fun Horse Facts for Kids**
- **Fun Bird Facts for Kids**
- **Fun Backyard Bird Facts for Kids**
- **Fun Dinosaur Facts for Kids**
- **Fun T-Rex Facts for Kids**

Made in the USA
Las Vegas, NV
15 December 2024

14517666R00050